CAMBRIDGE

A1 Movers 4

AUTHENTIC PRACTICE TESTS

STUDENT'S BOOK

WITHOUT ANSWERS

WITH AUDIO

Cambridge University Press
www.cambridge.org/elt

Cambridge Assessment English
www.cambridgeenglish.org

Information on this title: www.cambridge.org/9781009036245

First published 2022

20 19 18 17 16 15 14 13 12 11 10

Printed in Brazil by Forma Certa Grafica Digital LTDA

A catalogue record for this publication is available from the British Library

ISBN 978-1-009-03627-6 Student's Book with Answers with Audio with Resource Bank
ISBN 978-1-009-03624-5 Student's Book without Answers with Audio

The authors and publishers acknowledge the following sources of copyright material and are grateful for the permissions granted. While every effort has been made, it has not always been possible to identify the sources of all the material used, or to trace all copyright holders. If any omissions are brought to our notice, we will be happy to include the appropriate acknowledgements on reprinting and in the next update to the digital edition, as applicable.

Illustrations: Cambridge Assessment

Audio production by dsound recording studios

Typeset by QBS Learning

Cover illustration: Leo Trinidad/Astound

Contents

Part 1

– 5 questions –

Listen and draw lines. There is one example.

Julia Fred Peter Daisy

Paul Sally Jack

Part 2

– 5 questions –

Listening test audio

Listen and write. There is one example.

New toy shop!

	Name of new shop:	The ...Games Store...
1	Name of street:	.... Street
2	Shop closed on:	....
3	What Lily bought there:	a toy ....
4	Shop closes at:	.... o'clock
5	Colour of building:	....

Part 3

– 5 questions –

Listening test audio

Jim and his father have got to take lots of different things to different places today. Where do they have to take each thing?

Listen and write a letter in each box. There is one example.

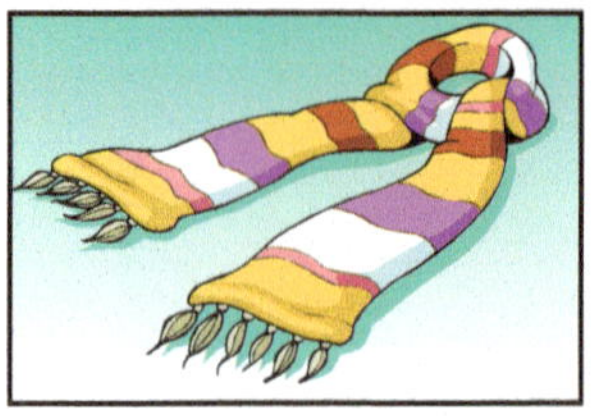

scarf [E]

comic [ ]

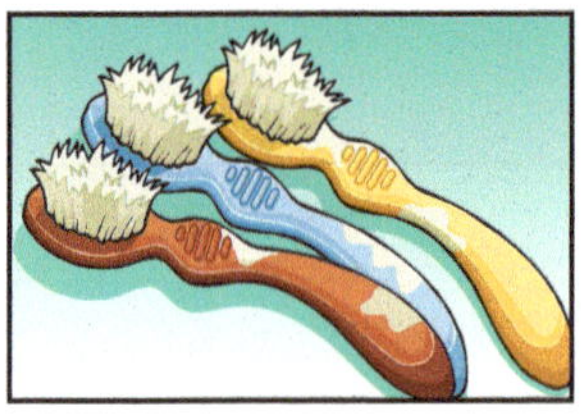

toothbrushes [ ]

cup [ ]

ticket [ ]

plant [ ]

A

B

C

D

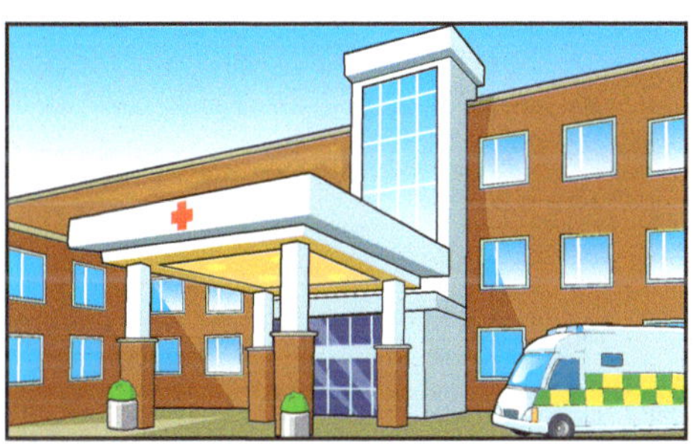

E

F

G

H

Part 4

– 5 questions –

Listening test audio

Listen and tick (✔) the box. There is one example.

What did Vicky see at the beach?

A ☑

B ☐

C ☐

1 Which are Mrs Field's favourite animals?

A ☐

B ☐

C ☐

2 What is the weather like outside now?

A ☐

B ☐

C ☐

3 What is Clare doing now?

A ☐

B ☐

C ☐

4 What is the matter with Dan?

A ☐

B ☐

C ☐

5 What do the man and the woman both want for lunch?

A ☐

B ☐

C ☐

Part 5

– 5 questions –

Listening test audio

Listen and colour and write. There is one example.

Blank Page

Part 1

– 5 questions –

Look and read. Choose the correct words and write them on the lines. There is one example.

Example

This animal is brown and it can hop very well. ......a kangaroo......

Questions

1 You stand in this when you want to wash your body. ....

2 This animal lives in the sea and likes swimming near boats. ....

3 This room is under the house. People often put old things there. ....

4 This animal sleeps in the day and flies at night. ....

5 When it's sunny, people often sit on chairs on this. ....

Part 2

– 6 questions –

Read the text and choose the best answer.

Example

Fred: Did you have a nice weekend at your grandparents' house?

Daisy:

A Me too.
(B) It was great, thanks.
C I'd like that.

Questions

1 **Fred:** How often do you go to your grandparents' house?

Daisy:

A Last week.
B At four o'clock.
C Every weekend.

2 **Fred:** Where do your grandparents live?

Daisy:
A It's not mine.
B I think I can.
C In the countryside.

3 **Fred:** What do you do at your grandparents' house?

Daisy:
A We talk and play games.
B It's in the playground.
C It's always windy there.

4 **Fred:** Have you got any friends near your grandparents' house?

Daisy:
A It's near a village.
B Two or three.
C Sorry, I don't know them.

5 **Fred:** Do you enjoy going to your grandparents' house?

Daisy:
A No, there aren't.
B Yes, I love it.
C I'm the best.

6 **Fred:** Did your mum drive to your grandparents' house?

Daisy:
A Yes, that's right.
B Shall I help?
C By train.

Part 3

– 6 questions –

Read the story. Choose a word from the box. Write the correct word next to numbers 1–5. There is one example.

Jane and Sally are best friends. It was Sally's birthday and Jane wanted to ....buy.......... her a really nice present but she didn't have any ideas. 'I know,' said her mum. 'How about a scarf? Sally needs one when she goes ice skating because it's always **(1)** ....'

'Brilliant! Let's get her an orange one. That's her favourite colour,' said Jane.

At the party, Jane, Sally and their friends played games and ate cheese sandwiches and drank **(2)** .... of lemonade.

Then, Sally **(3)** .... her presents. She got a new orange helmet and ice skates from her mum and dad. She got some orange socks and an orange **(4)** .... from her aunt. When Sally saw the orange scarf from Jane, she **(5)** .... 'Thank you, everyone! I love orange and now I have everything I need for ice skating!' said Sally.

Example

buy

sweater

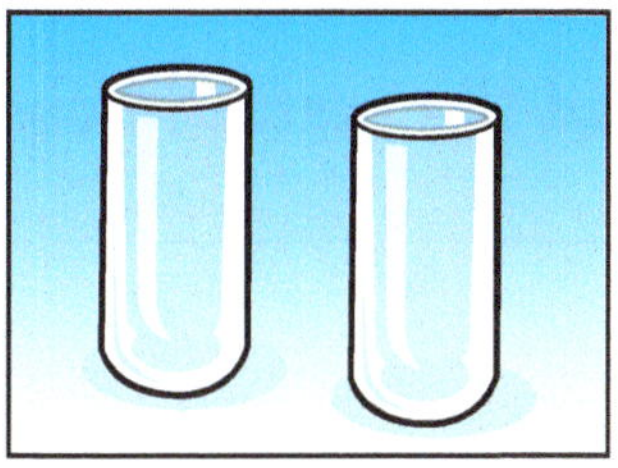

glasses

cold

curly

field

laughed

think

opened

(6) Now choose the best name for the story.

Tick one box.

Sally's new friend ☐

Sally goes ice skating ☐

Sally's presents ☐

Part 4

– 5 questions –

Read the text. Choose the right words and write them on the lines.

Penguins

Example There are ....many.............. kinds of penguin. Most penguins are black and white, and sometimes they are grey. They live in places

1 .... it snows a lot.

Some are very big and some are very small. They swim very

2 .... , but they can't fly.

3 Penguins .... eat meat. They like eating fish and they eat a lot of them every day.

4 They're good .... catching them in the sea.

When penguins swim and catch fish, they drink a lot of water.

You can see penguins in zoos all around the world. People love them

5 .... they are funny to watch.

Example	many	both	another
1	where	which	who
2	first	well	better
3	no	never	nothing
4	to	in	at
5	than	or	because

Part 5

– 7 questions –

Look at the pictures and read the story. Write some words to complete the sentences about the story. You can use 1, 2 or 3 words.

Jack's new pet

Jack loves all kinds of animals and he has lots of books about them. All of Jack's friends have a pet, but Jack hasn't got one. Peter has a big, black dog called Ben. Ben always sleeps outside on an old chair. Jack and Peter often take Ben to the park. Jack likes playing games there with Ben.

Examples

Jack loves animals, but he doesn't have a ....pet.................... .

Peter's dog has ....an old chair......... to sleep on.

Questions

1 Jack and Peter often go .... with Ben to play games.

Last Saturday, Mum and Jack went to the pet shop in their town. Jack loved the puppies, but Mum said, 'We can't get a puppy because we haven't got a garden.'

'What about a kitten?' asked Jack.

'Sorry,' said the man in the shop. 'A little girl bought the last one yesterday.'

2 On Saturday, Mum took Jack to the .... in their town.

3 Mum didn't want to get a dog because there isn't a

.... at the house.

4 They couldn't buy a .... because there weren't any in the shop.

Then, a red and yellow parrot said, 'Hello! I'm Vicky. What's your name?'

Jack was really surprised! 'Wow! This is a very clever bird. And I like her name, too. Can this be my new pet, please, Mum?' asked Jack.

'OK,' said Mum. 'Parrots are fun and you don't have to take them for a walk!'

They bought some food and a new cage for Vicky, and they took her home in it.

'Thank you, Mum! Vicky's a fantastic pet!'

'Yes, I am!' said Vicky.

5 The parrot was called ....

6 Jack was very .... when the parrot talked to him.

7 Vicky went home with Mum and Jack in a ....

Blank Page

Part 6

– 6 questions –

Look and read and write.

Examples

The people are in the ....hospital........ .

What's above the bed? ....a picture........

Questions

Complete the sentences.

1 The doctor is wearing a ....

2 The boy in the red T-shirt is holding ....

Answer the questions.

3 How many children are in bed?

....

4 What is on the table?

....

Now write two sentences about the picture.

5 ....

6 ....

Part 1

– 5 questions –

Listening test audio

Listen and draw lines. There is one example.

Charlie Daisy Jack Jane

Sally Fred Vicky

Part 2

– 5 questions –

Listening test audio

Listen and write. There is one example.

Peter's trip to the zoo

	Day of trip:	Wednesday
1	Travelled by:	....
2	Animals we saw:	Kangaroos and ....
3	Ate lunch:	at the .... café
4	Took a bottle of:	....
5	Teacher on trip:	Mr ....

Part 3

– 5 questions –

Listening test audio

Anna is telling her teacher about the food her friends like. What food does each person like?

Listen and write a letter in each box. There is one example.

Sue [B]

Hugo [ ]

Zoe [ ]

Bill [ ]

Matt [ ]

Grace [ ]

A

B

C

D

E

F

G

H

Part 4

– 5 questions –

Listening test audio

Listen and tick (✔) the box. There is one example.

What work does Jim do?

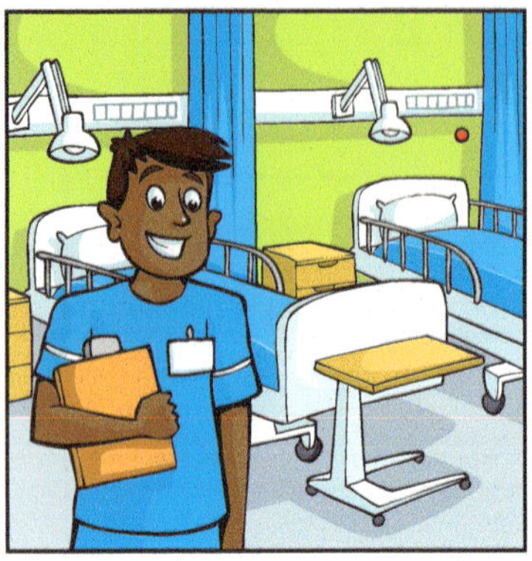

A ☐

B ☐

C ☑

1 Where is Mary's baseball cap?

A ☐

B ☐

C ☐

2 Which place did Dan learn about today in school?

A ☐

B ☐

C ☐

3 What is Lily doing now?

A ☐

B ☐

C ☐

4 Where did Paul see his grandma?

A ☐

B ☐

C ☐

5 What is Kim's favourite sport?

A ☐

B ☐

C ☐

Part 5

– 5 questions –

Listening test audio

Listen and colour and write. There is one example.

Blank Page

Part 1

– 5 questions –

Look and read. Choose the correct words and write them on the lines. There is one example.

a net

a shower

a balcony

roller skates

a café

coats

a scarf

a library

Example

You go to this place to look at books. ....a library..........

Questions

1 When you kick a football into this, you score a goal! ....

2 You wear this around your neck on cold days. ....

3 People sit here to have something to eat or drink. ....

4 You can stand under this and wash your hair. ....

5 When you put these on your feet, you can move really quickly! ....

Part 2

– 6 questions –

Read the text and choose the best answer.

Example

Peter:		What's your favourite sport, Lily?
Lily:	A	No, it's basketball.
	(B)	I like hockey a lot.
	C	It's fantastic. Let's dance.

Questions

1	**Peter:**		Do you like going to the sports centre?
	Lily:	A	Yes, I love it there.
		B	Yes, I must do that.
		C	Yes, please show me.

2 **Peter:** I enjoy going to the pool at the sports centre.

Lily:
A Good morning.
B Here you are.
C Me too.

3 **Peter:** Which days do you go swimming?

Lily:
A Not this week.
B Monday and Friday.
C It's after school.

4 **Peter:** Are you good at swimming?

Lily:
A I'm better at hockey.
B I'm really well, thanks.
C It's the best one.

5 **Peter:** When did you learn to swim?

Lily:
A I was all right yesterday.
B There were three of us.
C I was very young.

6 **Peter:** How about going for a swim now?

Lily:
A I know you are.
B I'm sorry, I can't.
C It's not my swimsuit.

Part 3

– 6 questions –

Read the story. Choose a word from the box. Write the correct word next to numbers 1–5. There is one example.

Jack, who was 11, woke his ....sister.......... up at 7 o'clock.

'Today is Mum's birthday,' he said. 'Let's make her some breakfast.'

Sally, who was only 5, **(1)** .... her hands.

'Great idea!' she said, and jumped out of bed.

'Shall we make her some soup?' she asked. 'Mum loves soup.

We can put carrots, apples and kiwis in it, and what about

(2) .... on the top?'

Jack laughed. 'Carrot soup is good, but we can't put fruit in soup. That's silly!' he said. 'Let's make pancakes. They're easier, I think! Let's make her a **(3)** .... of coffee, too.'

'OK,' Sally said, 'with some milk?'

'Yes!'

They **(4)** .... everything very carefully to their mother's bedroom. She was very surprised!

'What are you bringing me?' she asked.

'Your breakfast, Mum. It's our birthday **(5)** .... to you!' Sally said.

'Yes! Here you are! Happy birthday, Mum!' Jack said.

'Wow!' Mum answered. 'Pancakes and coffee! Thank you!'

Example

sister

film

carried

present

cough

clapped

cup

cooked

cheese

(6) Now choose the best name for the story.

Tick one box.

A happy morning for Mum! ☐

Jack eats a lot of food! ☐

Sally's mother has a good idea! ☐

Part 4

– 5 questions –

Read the text. Choose the right words and write them on the lines.

The moon

Example When you look up at the sky, on ....most........ nights when there are no clouds, you can see the moon. People can't

1 .... there because it's too cold at night and too hot in the day.

2 .... grows on the moon because it never rains

3 there, but we think the moon .... some water on it. There are lots of mountains on the moon. Some of them are really

4 .... ! On the internet you can see a video of the

5 first man .... walked on the moon.

Example	one	most	another
1	live	lived	living
2	Any	Both	Nothing
3	has	have	having
4	tallest	taller	tall
5	where	who	which

Part 5

– 7 questions –

Look at the pictures and read the story. Write some words to complete the sentences about the story. You can use 1, 2 or 3 words.

Mrs Sail's difficult morning!

Mrs Sail worked on the top floor of a big building in the city. She often went to work by train because she lived in the countryside.

But last Thursday, at the station, the man who worked there said, 'Sorry! There are no trains today! The driver is ill, and there's lots of snow.'

Mrs Sail wasn't happy!

'Well, I don't want to, but I must try and drive to work today,' she thought.

Examples

The big building where Mrs Sail ....worked.......... was in the city.

Mrs Sail often caught a train to work because her home was in

.......the countryside........ .

Questions

1 Mrs Sail couldn't travel by train last Thursday, because the

.... was sick.

2 Mrs Sail had to .... to work that morning.

But driving to the city was very slow because there was lots of snow on the road.

There was a car park opposite the building where Mrs Sail worked. But that morning, there were hundreds of cars in it.

'Oh no!' she thought. 'Where can I put my car today?'

She looked at her watch and started to drive around the busy city. Then she looked at all the pretty snow on the roofs and on the grass and she had an idea. She drove home again!

3 Mrs Sail had to drive slowly because the road to the city had

.... on it.

4 The .... that was opposite Mrs Sail's building had too many cars in it.

5 Mrs Sail didn't go to work that morning. She went

....

When they saw the car, Mary and Fred ran outside. 'Why aren't you at work today, Mum?' they asked.

'Because I want to have some fun with you! Go and get your coats! Come on! Let's all go to Lake Park!'

'Hooray!' the children said. 'We can go ice skating there!'

And they did.

6 .... were surprised to see Mrs Sail when she came home.

7 Mrs Sail's family went ice skating at .... that day.

Blank Page

Part 6

– 6 questions –

Look and read and write.

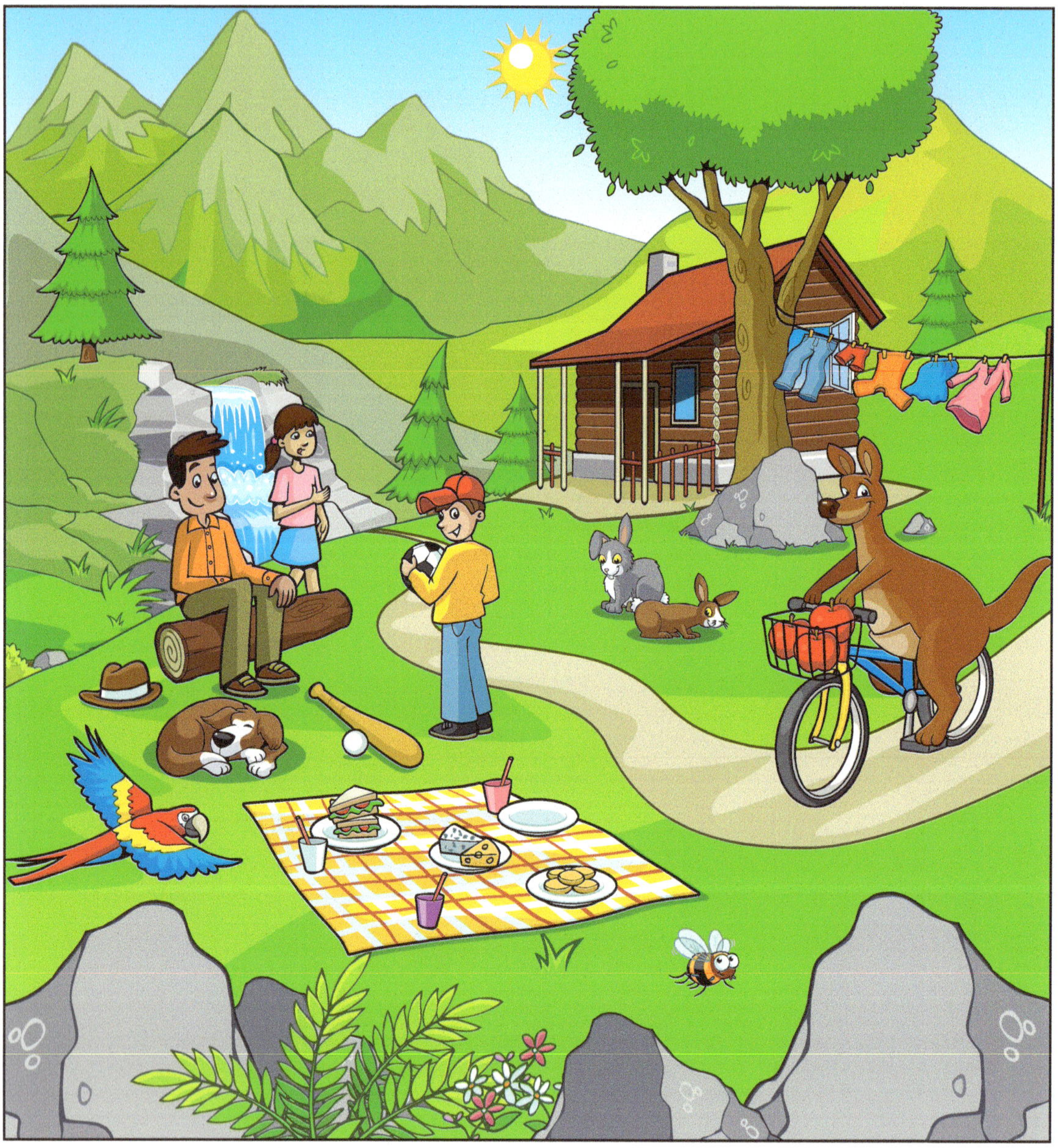

Examples

The man is wearing an orange ......shirt...... .

What is the weather like? ......It's sunny...... .

Questions

Complete the sentences.

1 The kangaroo is riding ....

2 The boy is holding ....

Answer the questions.

3 What is the parrot doing?

....

4 Which animal is asleep?

....

Now write two sentences about the picture.

5 ....

6 ....

Part 1

– 5 questions –

Listening test audio

Listen and draw lines. There is one example.

Peter Zoe Fred Lily

Charlie Jane Jack

Part 2

– 5 questions –

Listening test audio

Listen and write. There is one example.

Paul's new friend

Paul's friend's name: ....Jim............

1 Teacher's name: Mrs ....

2 Day Jim goes swimming: ....

3 Floor of Jim's apartment: ....

4 Drink at birthday party: ....

5 Kitten's name: ....

Part 3

– 5 questions –

Listening test audio

What work do the people in Mr Brown's family do?

Listen and write a letter in each box. There is one example.

his uncle [D]

his aunt [ ]

his brother [ ]

his sister [ ]

his cousin [ ]

his daughter [ ]

A

B

C

D

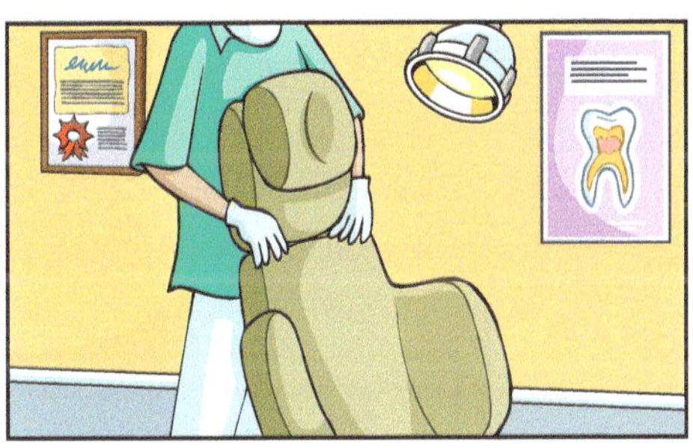

E

F

G

H

Part 4

– 5 questions –

Listening test audio

Listen and tick (✔) the box. There is one example.

Which is Julia's favourite day of the week?

A ✔

B ☐

C ☐

1 Where are Daisy's black shoes?

A ☐

B ☐

C ☐

2 What was the weather like in the mountains?

A ☐

B ☐

C ☐

3 What's the matter with Sally?

A ☐ **B** ☐ **C** ☐

4 Why is Vicky tired?

A ☐ **B** ☐ **C** ☐

5 Which present does Ben want to buy for his mum?

A ☐ **B** ☐ **C** ☐

Part 5

– 5 questions –

Listening test audio

Listen and colour and write. There is one example.

Blank Page

Part 1

– 5 questions –

Look and read. Choose the correct words and write them on the lines. There is one example.

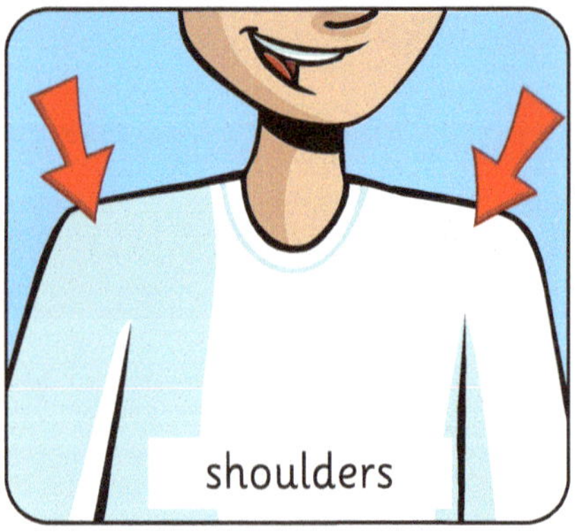

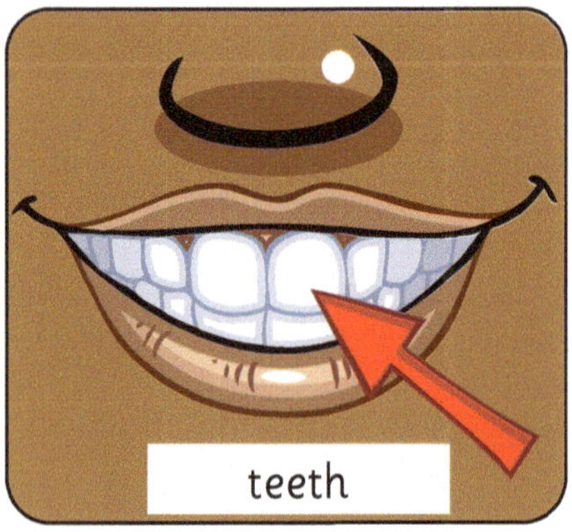

Example

Animals like pandas, penguins and lions sometimes live here. ....a zoo..........

Questions

1 You need these to eat and you have to clean them every day. ....

2 You can buy lots of different kinds of food here. ....

3 People go to this place to catch a train. ....

4 You have two of these and they are at the top of your arms. ....

5 Some men grow these on their faces. ....

Part 2

– 6 questions –

Read the text and choose the best answer.

Example

Charlie: Do you like your new house, Clare?

Clare:
A It's yours.
(B) Yes, it's great!
C I like that.

Questions

1 **Charlie:** Where do you live now?

Clare:
A Near the park.
B No, I don't.
C This is a town.

2 **Charlie:** Can you walk to school from your new house?

Clare:
A No, Mum's car is old.
B No, it's not my bike.
C No, I take the bus.

3 **Charlie:** When did you move to your new house?

Clare:
A At the weekend.
B It's my birthday.
C OK, at 5 o'clock.

4 **Charlie:** What's your new bedroom like?

Clare:
A There's a bedroom there.
B Next to the bathroom.
C It's bigger than my old one.

5 **Charlie:** Have you got a computer in your room?

Clare:
A No, you've got both of them.
B Yes, it's on my desk.
C OK, here you are.

6 **Clare:** Would you like to come and see my new house?

Charlie:
A I'd love to.
B That's not mine.
C It's the best one.

Part 3

– 6 questions –

Read the story. Choose a word from the box. Write the correct word next to numbers 1–5. There is one example.

Daisy and her Dad went into the town centre after

.............school............ yesterday.

They both wanted to buy a birthday **(1)** .... for Daisy's Mum.

Dad got her a scarf and Daisy found a book that Mum wanted.

'OK,' said Dad, 'Now let's get Mum a cake. Where can we buy one?'

'The best ones are in Mr Brown's café,' said Daisy. 'Right,' said Dad, 'but we must be quick. I need to go home to **(2)** .... Mum's birthday dinner.'

They went to the café and they chose a **(3)** .... cake.

When they got home Daisy said, 'Dad! I think our shopping bags are in the café. We didn't bring them home.'

'Oh no!' said Dad. 'It's 6 o'clock. The café is closed!'

'This is terrible!' Daisy said. 'We've got nothing to give Mum!'

Then Mum came home. 'I went to the café to get a

(4) .... of water,' she said. 'And Mr Brown gave me these shopping bags. Are they yours?'

Daisy and Dad **(5)** .... 'No, they're for you! Happy Birthday!' they said.

Example

school

cook

asleep

chocolate

present

climb

laughed

built

bottle

(6) Now choose the best name for the story.

Tick one box.

Dad's birthday ☐

Mr Brown buys a cake ☐

Mum's birthday present ☐

Part 4

– 5 questions –

Read the text. Choose the right words and write them on the lines.

Kangaroos

Example There are different kinds ....of.......... kangaroo.

There are red ones and brown ones. The red kangaroo is the biggest

1 one and it is often taller .... a person.

2 There are some kangaroos .... live in trees.

These are very small.

Kangaroos have big ears, long faces and very strong tails. They have

3 two long legs and two very short legs. They ....

hop like rabbits and they can jump very well. They are good

4 .... swimming, too.

5 Kangaroos .... not eat any meat. They only eat

grass and leaves.

Example	of	in	from
1	up	for	than
2	that	what	where
3	down	sometimes	outside
4	at	off	by
5	does	did	do

Part 5

– 7 questions –

Look at the pictures and read the story. Write some words to complete the sentences about the story. You can use 1, 2 or 3 words.

The new family on the farm

Julia and Peter always go to their grandparents' house at the weekend. Grandma and Grandpa have a farm and the children like to play there. Julia likes to help Grandma with the animals and Peter likes to ride on the tractor with Grandpa.

Last Saturday, when Grandma and Grandpa went into the house to make lunch, the children started to play a game. Julia hid in a place in the garden and Peter had to find her.

Examples

The children go to see their grandparents every ....weekend.......... .

Julia and Peter help their grandparents on ....the farm.......... a lot.

Questions

1 When their grandparents went inside to .... , the children played outside.

2 .... had to look for his sister in the garden.

Julia went to hide under the old tractor. There were some boxes near the tractor. Something moved in one of them. She called to her brother. 'Peter, look! What's in that box?'

The children looked into the box and they saw a mother cat with its three small kittens. Peter picked one up. 'They're really little!' he said.

3 Julia hid from Peter under .... , near some boxes.

4 When the children looked inside one of the boxes, they were surprised to see a .... with her three babies.

5 Peter held one of the .... in his hands.

Grandpa came to find the children. 'What are you doing?' he asked.

'Look, Grandpa!' said Peter. 'The cat has some kittens.'

'They're beautiful and they are all different,' said Julia. 'There's a black one, a white one and this one is grey.'

'I think they're hungry,' said Grandpa. 'Let's go and look for some food for them.'

'And for us!' said Peter.

6 The children showed the animals in the box to

....

7 The animals were hungry so Grandpa went to get some

.... for them.

Blank Page

Part 6

– 6 questions –

Look and read and write.

Examples

The grown-ups in the shop are both wearing ....sweaters.......... .

Where are all these people? ....in a shopping centre..........

Questions

Complete the sentences.

1 On the shortest girl's T-shirt there is a ....

2 The girl who is in the blue coat is looking in the

....

Answer the questions.

3 What is the boy who is sitting on the floor doing?

....

4 What is the man with the motorbike helmet wearing?

....

Now write two sentences about the picture.

5 ....

6 ....

Find the Differences

Picture Story

Jack finds his kitten

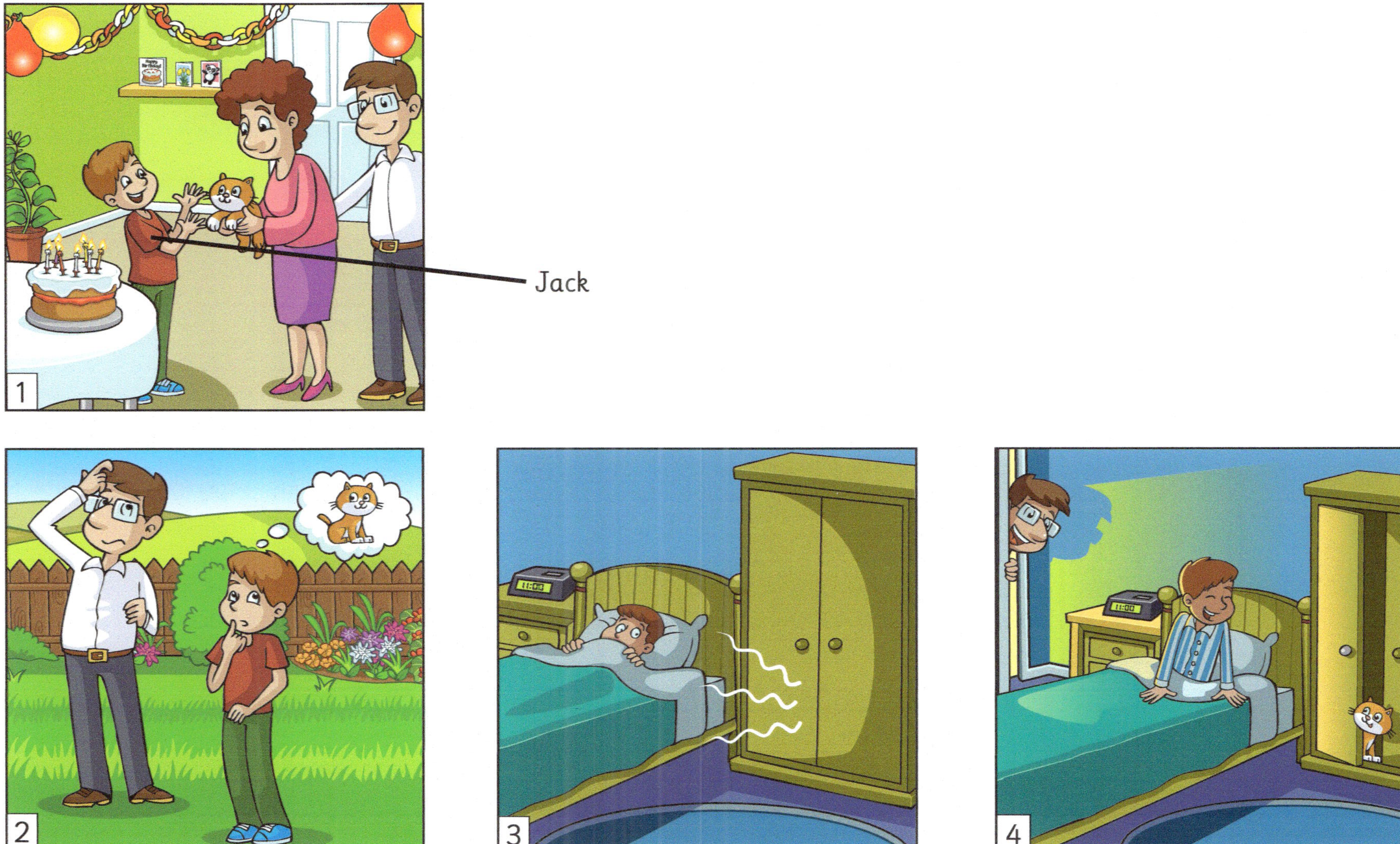

Odd-one-out

Blank Page

Find the Differences

Picture Story

Sally helps a kitten

Odd-one-out

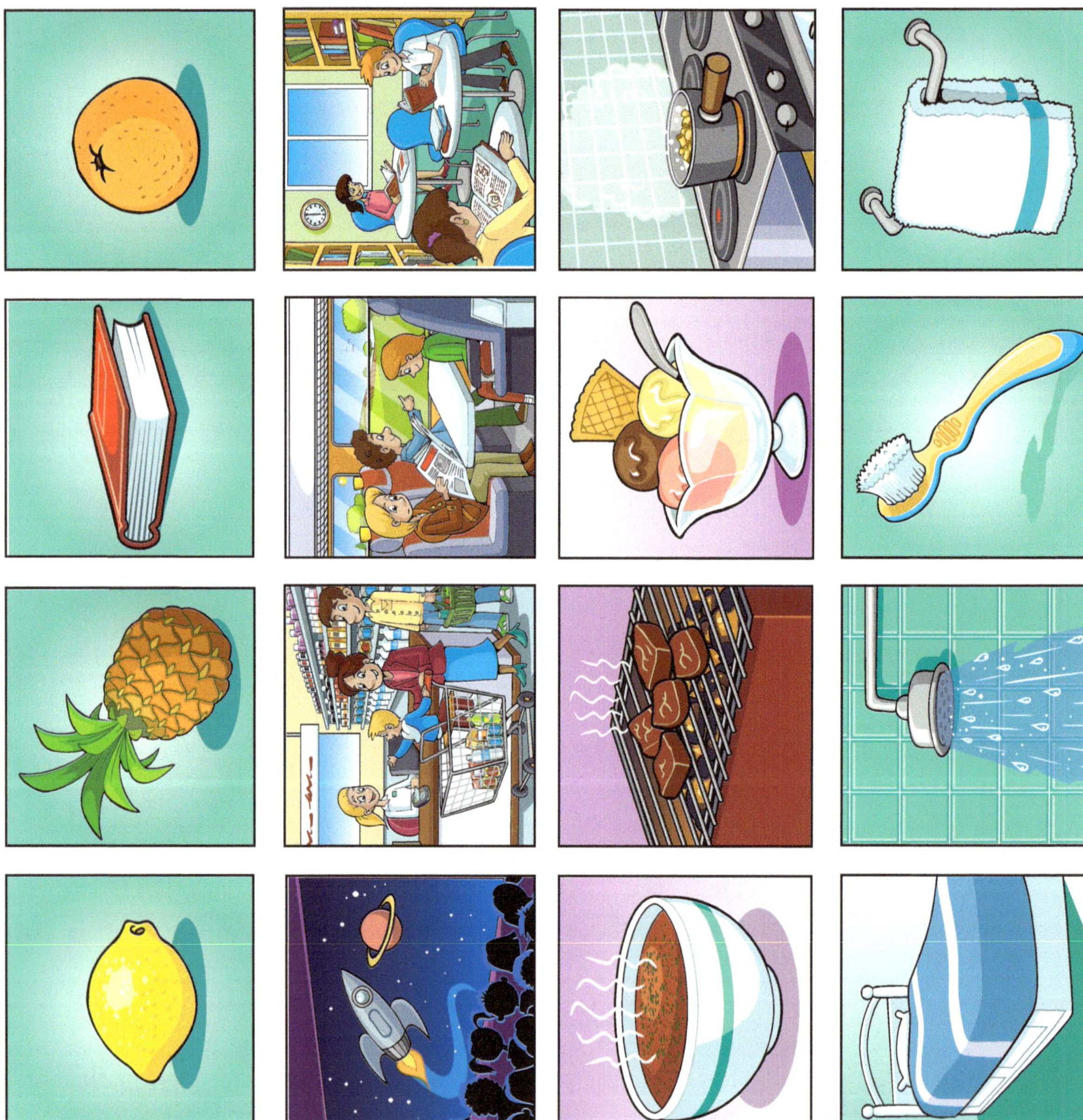

Blank Page

Find the Differences

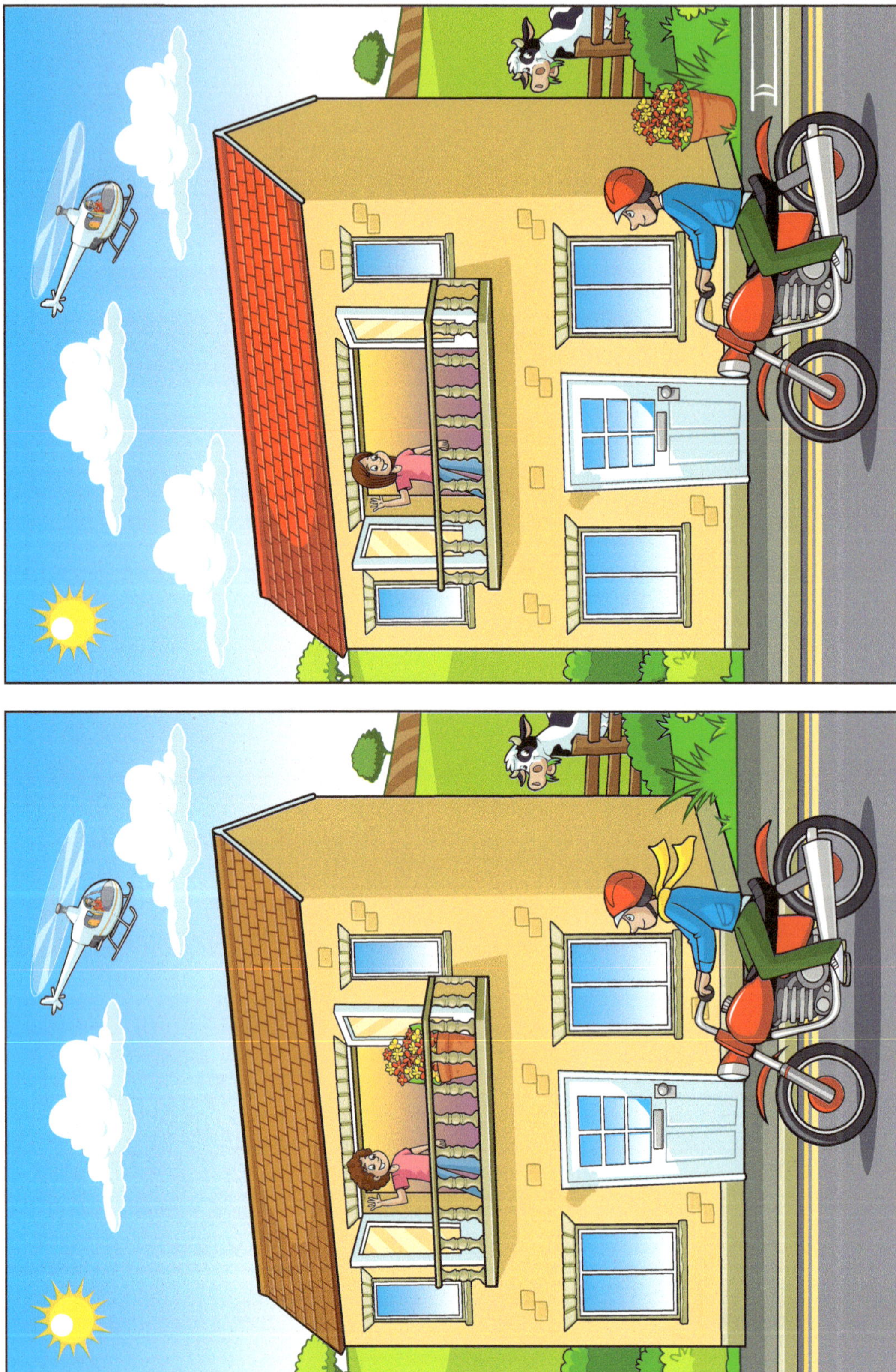

Picture Story

Charlie writes his homework

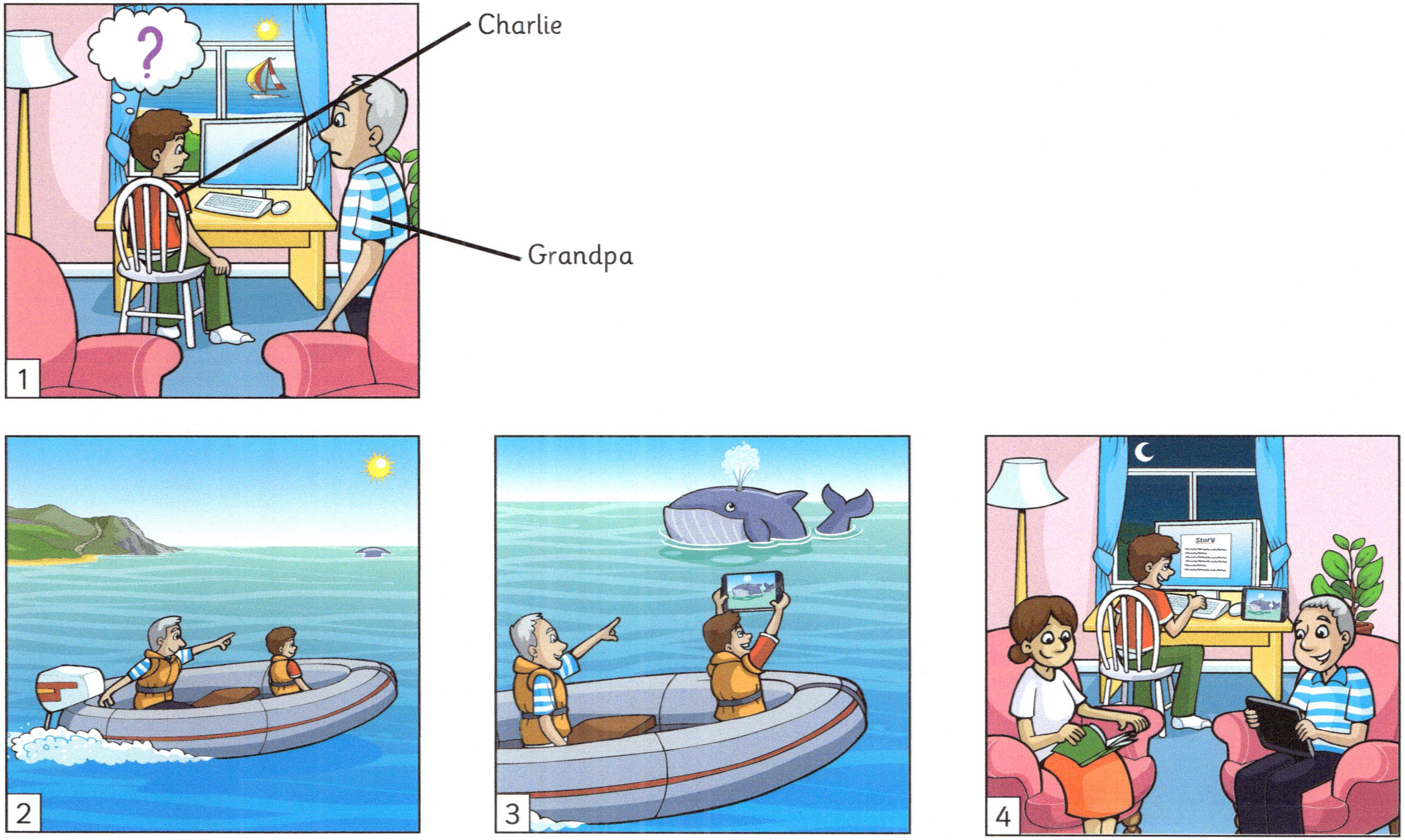

Odd-one-out